York

York

I ONLY LiKe WHaT I LiKe

BOLLiX
books

WORDS AND PICTURES BY **Julie Baer**

Printed in Singapore
FIRST EDITION
1 2 3 4 5 6 7 8 9 10

The illustrations were made with cut-paper collage, using found imagery and hand-painted rice paper.

Design by Julie Baer and Keith Warren

Library of Congress Cataloging-in-Publication Data

Baer, Julie.
I only like what I like / story and pictures by Julie Baer. – 1st ed.
p. cm.
Summary: Dewey Jackson Braintree-Berg only likes what he likes, but under some very special circumstances he might like something else.
ISBN 1-932188-00-2 (alk. paper)
[1. Choice–Fiction. 2. Growth–Fiction. 3. Jews–United States–Fiction.] I. Title.

PZ7.B1397 Iae 2003
[E]–dc21

2002013155

BOLLIX
books
www.bollixbooks.com

For Mookie (1988 - 2000)

Thank you, Tim, Luc, and Ike, Bette Baer, Caren Loebel-Fried, Jennifer Flannery, Staley Krause, and Keith Warren.

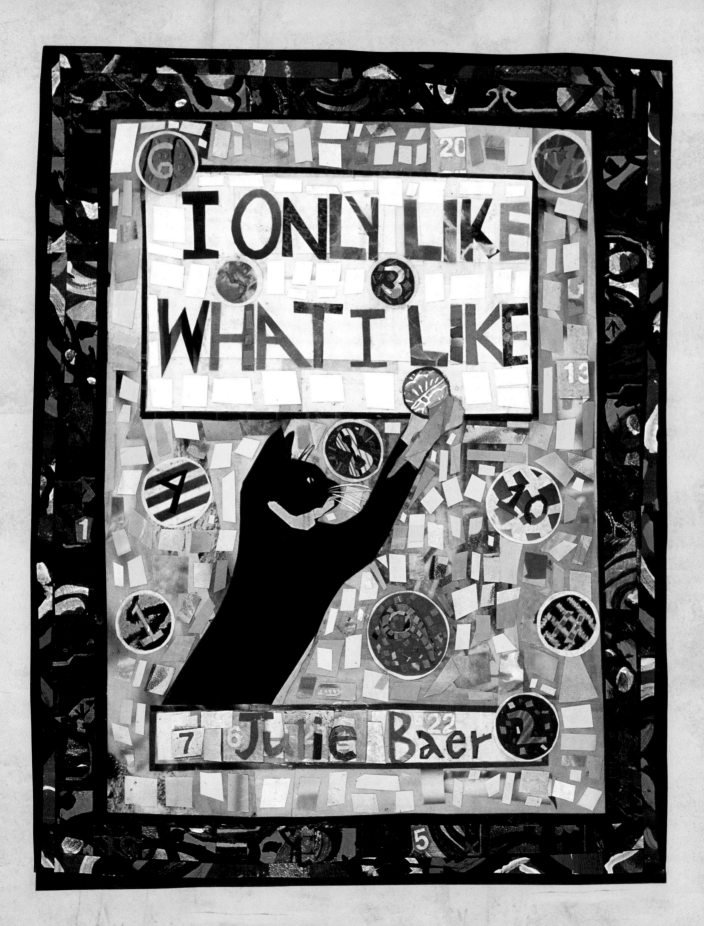

My full name is Dewey Jackson Braintree-Berg
and I only like what I like.

But on Sunday, Daddy and I were making a surprise breakfast
for Mommy, and we measured and sliced and stirred and poured and when we
finally opened up the waffle cooker, out came rectangles! I ate three!

And ten strawberries.

I only like noodles shaped like letters.

But on Monday, Irene and Nick invited us over for squiggly green macaroni.

(I pretended they were moray eels.)

Nicky let me shake the shake cheese

I only like red apples.

But Tuesday was Jewish New Year in our home, and Mommy and I cut up red and green and yellow apples and everybody dipped them in honey for a sweet new year.

I got to squeeze the honey bear!

I only like Jess to baby-sit for Abe and me. (I actually hate it when Mommy and Daddy go out because why can't they just stay home?)

But on Wednesday, Boppa came over and we popped corn and painted our faces and ran around outside until really really late, roaring and roaring!

(Mommy and Daddy came home way too early.)

I only like my brother-cat Mookie.

But on Thursday, the scary neighbor-cat wanted to play ball.

And man can that cat catch and throw!

I only like yellow and white houses like my yellow and white house.

But on Friday, we went over to Grandma May's to light the Friday night candles and eat Sabbath pizza. I got to ride in the elevator and even push the buttons to go up and to go down. We counted all the up and down numbers and listen to this:

Grandma's house has eleven floors!

I only like to sleep with the great big, bright light turned on for the whole, entire night. So don't even think about turning it off after I'm asleep.

(I can tell if Mommy switches it off even if I'm asleep because my dreams are darker. And Wee Wee will tell on Mommy.)

But now it's Saturday and Daddy just plugged in a night light which is a little seashell, and I switched it on, and it reminds me of the beach!

I'm turning off the bright light and now Peach and Wee Wee won't be scared anymore.

We like our new shining seashell.

I bet tonight I'll dream about the golden-apple seashore with baseball cats catching flying numbers, and popcorn faces with red and yellow and green swimming squiggles, and sweet rectangles in the morning when I wake up.

good night

Bollix Books is the name of the publishing company that made this book and had it put on the bookshelf at your store or library. Bollix is a funny kind of name, isn't it? It means to throw into disorder. Now why would a company name itself after a word that means to make a mess? Is Bollix Books disorderly? Well, sometimes but mostly not. Actually, the people at Bollix believe that when folks experience new, unusual, unexpected and sometimes disorderly things in their lives, they learn and they grow. That's why kids are always having such a good time, because they've only been around for 5 or 7 or maybe 8 years and pretty much every day they encounter something that they didn't expect. That's also why adults, who hardly ever get to experience new things, can be pretty boring and get so tired sometimes. Bollix wants to make books that don't fall into the normal order of things so that children can continue to be full of energy and enthusiasm and so the adults who read to them can say to themselves, "Hmmmm, that's not the normal way of doing things!" Or maybe they'll say, "I don't like it!" or better yet, "Wow, how very unusual." Either way, we hope they'll brighten up a little bit!

Bollix Books is just getting started. We're a baby company, you might say. And we've been so busy putting this book together (along with a few others), that we've not had time to do something very important. We've not had time to figure out how we can help people. Your parents probably tell you how important it is to help people, and our parents do too. One thing that we know is that we'd like to set aside some of the money we earn each time we sell a book and give it to people who really need it. And we'd like to ask you, the enthusiastic ones, if you have any great plans or thoughts about where that money should go and how it should be used.

Some people think that kids can't do anything because they are too small, but we disagree. We think children have the most giving hearts and the best ideas. So, please write to us at our website www.bollixbooks.com